Grandma's
CLASSIC RECIPES™

Publications International, Ltd.

Microwave Cooking: Microwave ovens vary in wattage. Use the cooking times as guidelines and check for doneness before adding more time.

Preparation/Cooking Times: Preparation times are based on the approximate amount of time required to assemble the recipe before cooking, baking, chilling or serving. These times include preparation steps such as measuring, chopping and mixing. The fact that some preparations and cooking can be done simultaneously is taken into account. Preparation of optional ingredients and serving suggestions is not included.

Table of Contents

Farm-Fresh Starts

Nothing could get you out of bed faster than the wonderful aromas coming from Grandma's kitchen. Now you can make those same dishes to greet your own family in the morning.

Summer Sausage 'n' Egg Wedges

    4 eggs, beaten

    $^1/_3$ cup milk

    $^1/_4$ cup all-purpose flour

    $^1/_2$ teaspoon baking powder

    $^1/_8$ teaspoon garlic powder

  2$^1/_2$ cups (10 ounces) shredded Cheddar or mozzarella cheese,
      divided

  1$^1/_2$ cups diced HILLSHIRE FARM® Summer Sausage

    1 cup cream-style cottage cheese with chives

Preheat oven to 375°F.

Combine eggs, milk, flour, baking powder and garlic powder in medium bowl; beat until combined. Stir in 2 cups Cheddar cheese, Summer Sausage and cottage cheese. Pour into greased 9-inch pie plate. Bake, uncovered, 25 to 30 minutes or until golden and knife inserted into center comes out clean. To serve, cut into 6 wedges. Sprinkle wedges with remaining $^1/_2$ cup Cheddar cheese. *Makes 6 servings*

To help prevent eggs from absorbing odors from
other foods, refrigerate them in the original carton.
For best flavor, use eggs within a week of purchase.

Apple & Raisin Oven Pancake

1 large baking apple, cored and thinly sliced
$^1/_3$ cup golden raisins
2 tablespoons packed brown sugar
$^1/_2$ teaspoon ground cinnamon
4 eggs
$^2/_3$ cup milk
$^2/_3$ cup all-purpose flour
2 tablespoons butter or margarine, melted
Powdered sugar (optional)

Preheat oven to 350°F. Spray 9-inch pie plate with nonstick cooking spray.

Combine apple, raisins, brown sugar and cinnamon in medium bowl. Transfer to prepared pie plate.

Bake, uncovered, 10 to 15 minutes or until apple begins to soften. Remove from oven. *Increase oven temperature to 450°F.*

Meanwhile, whisk eggs, milk, flour and butter in medium bowl until blended. Pour batter over apple mixture.

Bake 15 minutes or until pancake is golden brown. Invert onto serving dish. Sprinkle with powdered sugar, if desired. *Makes 6 servings*

Apple & Raisin Oven Pancake

Sunrise Squares

1 pound BOB EVANS® Original Recipe Roll Sausage

2 slices bread, cut into ¹/₂-inch cubes (about 2 cups)

1 cup (4 ounces) shredded sharp Cheddar cheese

6 eggs

2 cups milk

¹/₂ teaspoon salt

¹/₂ teaspoon dry mustard

Preheat oven to 350°F. Crumble sausage into medium skillet. Cook over medium heat until browned, stirring occasionally. Drain off any drippings. Spread bread cubes in greased 11×7-inch baking dish; top with sausage and cheese. Whisk eggs, milk, salt and mustard until well blended; pour over cheese. Bake 30 to 40 minutes or until set. Let stand 5 minutes before cutting into squares; serve hot. Refrigerate leftovers.

Makes 6 servings

Tip: You can make this tasty meal ahead and refrigerate overnight before baking.

Serving Suggestion: Serve squares between toasted English muffins.

Vegetable Medley Quiche

Nonstick cooking spray

2 cups frozen diced potatoes with onions and peppers, thawed

1 can (10³/4 ounces) reduced-fat condensed cream of mushroom soup, divided

1 (16-ounce) package frozen mixed vegetables (such as zucchini, carrots and beans), thawed and drained

1 cup cholesterol-free egg substitute *or* 4 eggs

¹/2 cup grated Parmesan cheese, divided

¹/4 cup fat-free (skim) milk

¹/4 teaspoon dried dill weed

¹/4 teaspoon dried thyme leaves

¹/4 teaspoon dried oregano leaves

Dash salt and pepper

Preheat oven to 400°F. Spray 9-inch pie plate with nonstick cooking spray; press potatoes onto bottom and side of pan to form crust. Spray potatoes lightly with nonstick cooking spray. Bake 15 minutes.

Combine half of soup, mixed vegetables, egg substitute and half of cheese in small bowl; mix well. Pour egg mixture into potato shell; sprinkle with remaining cheese. *Reduce oven to 375°F.* Bake 35 to 40 minutes or until set.

Combine remaining soup, milk and seasonings in small saucepan; mix well. Simmer over low heat 5 minutes or until heated through. Serve sauce with quiche. *Makes 6 servings*

11

Ham and Cheese Bread Pudding

1 small loaf (8 ounces) sourdough, country French or Italian
    bread, cut into 1-inch-thick slices
3 tablespoons butter or margarine, softened
8 ounces ham or smoked ham, cubed
2 cups (8 ounces) shredded mild or sharp Cheddar cheese
3 eggs
2 cups milk
1 teaspoon dry mustard
$^1/_2$ teaspoon salt
$^1/_8$ teaspoon white pepper

1. Grease 11×7-inch baking dish. Spread 1 side of each bread slice with butter. Cut into 1-inch cubes; place on bottom of prepared dish. Top with ham; sprinkle with cheese.

2. Beat eggs in medium bowl. Whisk in milk, mustard, salt and pepper. Pour egg mixture evenly over bread mixture. Cover; refrigerate at least 6 hours or overnight.

3. Preheat oven to 350°F.

4. Bake bread pudding uncovered 45 to 50 minutes or until puffed and golden brown and knife inserted in center comes out clean. Garnish, if desired. Cut into squares. Serve immediately.   *Makes 8 servings*

Ham and Cheese Bread Pudding

Waffles with Strawberry Sauce

2¼ cups all-purpose flour

2 tablespoons sugar

1 tablespoon baking powder

½ teaspoon salt

2 eggs, beaten

¼ cup vegetable oil

2 cups milk

Strawberry Sauce (recipe follows)

1. Preheat waffle iron; grease lightly.

2. Sift flour, sugar, baking powder and salt into large bowl. Combine eggs, oil and milk in medium bowl. Stir liquid ingredients into dry ingredients until moistened.

3. For each waffle, pour about ¾ cup batter into waffle iron. Close lid and bake until steaming stops.* Serve with Strawberry Sauce.

Makes about 6 round waffles

Check the manufacturer's directions for recommended amount of batter and baking time.

Strawberry Sauce

1 pint strawberries, hulled

2 to 3 tablespoons sugar

1 tablespoon strawberry- or orange-flavored liqueur (optional)

Combine strawberries, sugar and liqueur in blender or food processor. Cover; process until smooth.

Makes 1½ cups

Waffle with Strawberry Sauce

Apple Brunch Strata

$^1/_2$ pound sausage, casing removed

4 cups cubed French bread

2 cups diced peeled Michigan Apples

$^1/_4$ cup sliced green onion

$^1/_3$ cup sliced black olives

1 $^1/_2$ cups (6 ounces) shredded sharp Cheddar cheese

2 cups reduced-fat milk

8 eggs

2 teaspoons spicy brown mustard

$^1/_2$ teaspoon salt

$^1/_4$ teaspoon black pepper

Paprika

1. Brown sausage in skillet over medium-high heat. Drain; set aside.

2. Spray 13×9×2-inch baking dish with nonstick cooking spray. Layer half of bread cubes in bottom of dish. Crumble sausage over bread. Top with Michigan Apples, green onion, olives and cheese. Place remaining bread on top.

3. Mix milk, eggs, mustard, salt and pepper in medium bowl; pour over bread. Cover with foil and refrigerate 4 hours or overnight.

4. Preheat oven to 350°F. Bake, covered, 45 minutes. Remove foil and bake 15 minutes or until center is set. Let stand 15 minutes before serving. Sprinkle with paprika, if desired. *Makes 8 servings*

Suggested Michigan Apple varieties to use: Empire, Gala, Golden Delicious, Ida Red, Jonagold, Jonathan, McIntosh or Rome.

Favorite recipe from **Michigan Apple Committee**

*When making a soufflé, gently fold the beaten egg
whites into the yolk mixture just until combined. Too
much agitation can cause the egg whites to break
down and the soufflé to fall.*

Ham & Cheese Grits Soufflé

3 cups water

$^3/_4$ cup quick-cooking grits

$^1/_2$ teaspoon salt

$^1/_2$ cup (2 ounces) shredded mozzarella cheese

2 ounces ham, finely chopped

2 tablespoons minced chives

2 eggs, separated

Dash hot pepper sauce

1. Preheat oven to 375°F. Grease 1$^1/_2$-quart soufflé dish or deep
casserole.

2. Bring water to a boil in medium saucepan. Stir in grits and salt. Cook,
stirring frequently, about 5 minutes or until thickened. Stir in cheese,
ham, chives, egg yolks and hot pepper sauce.

3. In small clean bowl, beat egg whites until stiff but not dry; fold into
grits mixture. Pour into prepared dish. Bake about 30 minutes or until
puffed and golden. Serve immediately.   *Makes 4 to 6 servings*

Southern Caramel Pecan Rolls

TOPPING

$^2/_3$ cup sifted powdered sugar

$^2/_3$ cup dark brown sugar

$^1/_2$ cup whipping cream

1 teaspoon vanilla

WESSON® No-Stick Cooking Spray

1 cup coarsely chopped pecans

ROLLS

1 cup dark raisins

$^1/_3$ cup brandy

2 (1-pound) loaves frozen sweet or white bread dough, thawed, but not doubled in size

$^1/_4$ cup WESSON® Best Blend Oil

$^1/_2$ cup packed dark brown sugar

1 tablespoon ground cinnamon

$^1/_2$ teaspoon ground nutmeg

Topping

In a medium bowl, stir together sugars, whipping cream and vanilla. Spray two 9×1$^1/_2$-inch round cake pans with Wesson® Cooking Spray. Evenly divide mixture between pans and sprinkle with pecans; set aside pans.

Rolls

In a small bowl, soak raisins in brandy for 30 minutes; set aside and stir occasionally.

On floured surface, roll *each* loaf into 12×8×¼-inch rectangle.
Generously brush *each* sheet of dough with Wesson® Oil. In a small bowl,
mix together sugar, cinnamon and nutmeg. Sprinkle over dough; top with
soaked raisins. Roll up rectangles jelly-roll style starting with long edge.
Pinch dough to seal. Cut into 12 slices. Place rolls, spiral side down, in
cake pans. Cover with towels and let rise in warm place for 30 minutes or
until nearly double in size. Preheat oven to 375°F. Bake, uncovered, for
15 to 20 minutes. Cover pans with foil to prevent overbrowning and bake
an additional 10 minutes. Cool in pans 7 minutes. Invert onto serving
plate. Best when served warm.   *Makes 24 rolls*

Southern Caramel Pecan Rolls

Garden Omelet

3 teaspoons butter or margarine, divided

$^1/_3$ cup chopped onion

$^1/_3$ cup chopped red bell pepper

$^1/_2$ cup sliced mushrooms

$^1/_2$ teaspoon dried basil leaves

4 eggs, beaten

1 tablespoon milk

$^1/_4$ teaspoon black pepper

Dash salt

$^1/_2$ cup (2 ounces) shredded Swiss cheese

1. Melt 1 teaspoon butter in large nonstick skillet over medium heat. Cook and stir onion and bell pepper 2 to 3 minutes or until onion is tender. Add mushrooms and basil; cook and stir 3 to 5 minutes more. Remove from skillet and keep warm.

2. Whisk together eggs, milk, black pepper and salt in medium bowl. Melt remaining 2 teaspoons butter in same skillet over medium heat; rotate pan to coat bottom. Pour egg mixture into skillet. Cook over medium heat; as eggs begin to set, gently lift edges of omelet with spatula and tilt skillet so that uncooked portion flows underneath.

3. When eggs are fully cooked, spoon vegetable mixture over half of omelet. Sprinkle with cheese. Loosen omelet with spatula and fold in half. Transfer to warm serving plate. *Makes 2 servings*

Prep and Cook Time: 20 minutes

Hash Brown Frittata

1 (10-ounce) package BOB EVANS® Skinless Link Sausage

6 eggs

1 (12-ounce) package frozen hash brown potatoes, thawed

1 cup (4 ounces) shredded Cheddar cheese

$^1/_3$ cup whipping cream

$^1/_4$ cup chopped green and/or red bell pepper

$^1/_4$ teaspoon salt

   Dash black pepper

Preheat oven to 350°F. Cut sausage into bite-size pieces. Cook in small skillet over medium heat until lightly browned, stirring occasionally. Drain off any drippings. Whisk eggs in medium bowl; stir in sausage and remaining ingredients. Pour into greased 2-quart casserole dish. Bake, uncovered, 30 minutes or until eggs are almost set. Let stand 5 minutes before cutting into squares; serve hot. Refrigerate leftovers.

Makes 6 servings

Hearty Soups & Stews

Take the chill out of a cold day with a piping-hot bowl of homemade soup or stew—just like Grandma used to make. Add some fresh warm bread and it's a comforting and filling meal.

Quick and Easy Sausage Stew

1 package (12 ounces) HEBREW NATIONAL® Beef Polish
    Sausage, cut into 1-inch slices

1 large onion, chopped

2 cloves garlic, minced

1 red bell pepper, seeded, cut into 1-inch pieces

1 green bell pepper, seeded, cut into 1-inch pieces

1 medium zucchini, cut into $1/2$-inch slices

8 ounces fresh mushrooms, thickly sliced

2 cans ($14^{1}/_2$ ounces each) stewed tomatoes, undrained

1 teaspoon dried basil leaves

$1/4$ teaspoon crushed red pepper

$1/4$ teaspoon salt

Cook sausage, onion and garlic in large deep nonstick skillet over medium-high heat 3 minutes. Add bell peppers, zucchini and mushrooms; cook 5 minutes, stirring occasionally.

Add stewed tomatoes with liquid, basil, crushed pepper and salt. Bring to a boil. Reduce heat. Cover; simmer 25 minutes, stirring occasionally.

Makes 6 servings

Chicken Vegetable Soup

1 bag SUCCESS® Rice
5 cups chicken broth
1 1/2 cups chopped uncooked chicken
1 cup sliced celery
1 cup sliced carrots
1/2 cup chopped onion
1/4 cup chopped fresh parsley
1/2 teaspoon black pepper
1/2 teaspoon dried thyme leaves, crushed
1 bay leaf
1 tablespoon lime juice

Prepare rice according to package directions.

Combine broth, chicken, celery, carrots, onion, parsley, pepper, thyme and bay leaf in large saucepan or Dutch oven. Bring to a boil over medium-high heat, stirring once or twice. Reduce heat to low; simmer 10 to 15 minutes or until chicken is no longer pink in center. Remove bay leaf; discard. Stir in rice and lime juice. Garnish, if desired.

Makes 4 servings

*To chop fresh parsley easily, after washing, pat it
dry with a paper towel and snip it into small pieces
with kitchen shears.*

Chicken Vegetable Soup

Potato-Cheese Soup

2 cups water

2 cups red potatoes, peeled and cut into cubes

3 tablespoons butter or margarine

1 small onion, finely chopped

3 tablespoons all-purpose flour

   Creole seasoning to taste

   Ground red pepper to taste

   Black pepper to taste

3 cups milk

1 cup (4 ounces) shredded Cheddar cheese

1 1/2 cups cubed cooked ham

   Chopped fresh parsley for garnish

1. Bring water to a boil in large saucepan over medium-high heat. Add potatoes and cook until tender, 13 to 15 minutes.

2. Meanwhile, melt butter in large skillet over medium heat. Add onion; cook and stir 4 to 5 minutes until onion is tender but not brown. Add flour. Season with Creole seasoning, red pepper and black pepper; cook and stir 3 to 4 minutes. Set aside.

3. Drain potatoes, reserving 1 cup liquid. (Add water to make 1 cup, if necessary.)

4. Gradually add potatoes, reserved liquid and milk to onion mixture; stir well.

5. Add cheese and ham. Reduce heat to low. Simmer 30 minutes, stirring frequently. Garnish, if desired. *Makes 12 servings*

Tomato, Chicken and Mushroom Soup

$^1/_4$ pound mushrooms, sliced*

1 tablespoon butter *or* margarine

2 cans (13$^3/_4$ ounces each) ready-to-serve chicken broth

2 cups diced cooked chicken

1 can (14$^1/_2$ ounces) whole tomatoes

1 can (8 ounces) tomato sauce

1 carrot, thinly sliced

1 envelope GOOD SEASONS® Italian Salad Dressing Mix

$^1/_4$ cup MINUTE® Original Rice, uncooked

*Substitute 1 jar (4$^1/_2$ ounces) sliced mushrooms, drained, for fresh mushrooms.

COOK and stir mushrooms in hot butter in large saucepan. Gradually stir in broth.

ADD chicken, tomatoes, tomato sauce, carrot and salad dressing mix. Bring to a boil. Reduce heat to low; cover. Simmer 10 minutes.

STIR in rice; cover. Remove from heat. Let stand 5 minutes.

Makes 8 servings

Prep Time: 10 minutes
Cook Time: 15 minutes plus standing

27

Creamy Clam Chowder

2$\frac{1}{2}$ cups water, divided

20 fresh hard-shell clams,* scrubbed and soaked

2 strips thick-sliced bacon

1 medium onion, chopped

1 rib celery, diced

4 tablespoons all-purpose flour

1 clove garlic, minced

3 medium red potatoes, peeled and diced

2 bay leaves

1 teaspoon salt

$\frac{1}{8}$ teaspoon black pepper

2 cups half-and-half

1 cup milk

Oyster crackers and lemon slices for garnish

*If fresh clams in shells are not available, substitute $\frac{3}{4}$ to 1 cup shucked clams. Omit step 1.

1. Place 1 cup water in large stockpot. Bring to a boil over high heat. Add clams. Cover stockpot; reduce heat to medium. Steam 5 to 7 minutes or until clams start to open. Remove clams from stockpot as they open. Discard any clams that remain unopened.

2. Remove clams from shells. Chop clams; set aside. (For shucked clams, drain and chop clams; set aside.)

3. Cook bacon in large saucepan over medium-high heat until crisp. Remove bacon to paper towels, leaving drippings in pan. Crumble bacon when cool enough to handle.

Creamy Clam Chowder

4. Add onion, celery, flour and garlic to bacon drippings and cook over medium heat, stirring occasionally, about 2 minutes or until vegetables are crisp-tender. Remove from heat.

5. Add potatoes to onion mixture. Stir in remaining 1 ½ cups water, bay leaves, salt and pepper. Bring to a boil over high heat. Reduce heat to medium-low; simmer, uncovered, until potatoes are tender, about 10 minutes.

6. Stir in half-and-half, milk and chopped clams; heat through over medium heat, stirring occasionally. (Or, stir in half-and-half, milk and chopped shucked clams; simmer over medium heat until clams are cooked.) Discard bay leaves. Stir in bacon. Serve with oyster crackers, if desired.   *Makes 6 servings*

Tuna Chowder

1 pound yellowfin tuna steaks, skinned and cubed

1 can (10³/₄ ounces) low-sodium chicken broth

1 soup can water

1 cup diced potatoes

¹/₂ cup each chopped onion, carrots and celery

¹/₂ cup frozen corn

¹/₂ teaspoon dried basil

¹/₄ teaspoon dried thyme

¹/₂ cup low-fat milk

1 tablespoon chopped parsley

Mix broth with 1 can of water in large saucepan; add potatoes. Bring to a boil over high heat. Reduce heat to low. Cover and simmer 10 to 15 minutes until potatoes are fork-tender.

Remove cooked potatoes from broth, reserving liquid. Purée cooked potatoes with ¹/₄ cup broth.

Add tuna, vegetables, seasonings and puréed potatoes to remaining broth in saucepan. Cover; simmer 8 to 10 minutes until fish flakes easily when tested with a fork and vegetables are tender.

Stir in milk. Heat to serving temperature; do not boil. Sprinkle with parsley just before serving. *Makes 4 servings*

Favorite recipe from **National Fisheries Institute**

Brunswick Stew

2 pounds chicken pieces, rinsed

$2^1/_3$ cups cold water, divided

1 can ($14^1/_2$ ounces) tomatoes, cut-up and undrained

2 large ribs celery, sliced

1 medium onion, chopped

2 cloves garlic, minced

1 bay leaf

$^1/_2$ teaspoon salt

$^1/_8$ teaspoon ground red pepper

6 small upeeled new potatoes (about $^3/_4$ pound), cut in half

1 cup frozen succotash (about $^1/_2$ of 10-ounce package)

1 cup cubed ham

1 tablespoon all-purpose flour

1. Combine chicken, 2 cups cold water, tomatoes with juice, celery, onion, garlic, bay leaf, salt and red pepper in 5-quart Dutch oven. Bring to a boil over high heat. Reduce heat to medium-low; simmer, uncovered, 45 minutes or until chicken is tender, skimming foam that rises to top.

2. Remove chicken from broth and let cool slightly. Discard bay leaf. Skim fat from soup. Remove chicken meat from bones; discard skin and bones. Cut chicken into bite-size pieces.

3. Add potatoes, succotash and ham to Dutch oven. Bring to a boil. Reduce heat; simmer, uncovered, 20 minutes or until potatoes are tender. Stir in chicken.

4. Stir flour into remaining $^1/_3$ cup cold water until smooth. Stir into stew. Cook and gently stir over medium heat until bubbly.   *Makes 6 servings*

Split Pea Soup

1 package (16 ounces) dried green or yellow split peas
1 pound smoked pork hocks *or* 4 ounces smoked sausage links,
    sliced and quartered *or* 1 meaty ham bone
7 cups water
1 medium onion, chopped
2 medium carrots, chopped
$^3/_4$ teaspoon salt
$^1/_2$ teaspoon dried basil leaves
$^1/_4$ teaspoon dried oregano leaves
$^1/_4$ teaspoon black pepper
    Ham and carrot strips for garnish

Rinse peas thoroughly in colander under cold running water, picking out any debris or blemished peas. Place peas, pork hocks and water in 5-quart Dutch oven.

Add onion, carrots, salt, basil, oregano and pepper to Dutch oven. Bring to a boil over high heat. Reduce heat to medium-low; simmer, uncovered, 1 hour 15 minutes or until peas are tender, stirring occasionally. Stir frequently near end of cooking to keep soup from scorching.

Remove pork hocks; cool. Cut meat into bite-size pieces.

Carefully ladle 3 cups hot soup into food processor or blender; cover and process until mixture is smooth.

Return puréed soup and meat to Dutch oven. (If soup is too thick, add a little water until desired consistency is reached.) Heat through. Ladle into bowls. Garnish, if desired. *Makes 6 servings*

Split Pea Soup

Vegetable Soup

2 tablespoons FILIPPO BERIO® Olive Oil

2 medium potatoes, peeled and quartered

2 medium onions, sliced

3 cups beef broth

8 ounces fresh green beans, trimmed and cut into 1-inch pieces

3 carrots, peeled and chopped

8 ounces fresh spinach, washed, drained, stemmed and chopped

1 green bell pepper, diced

2 tablespoons chopped fresh parsley

1 tablespoon chopped fresh basil *or* 1 teaspoon dried basil leaves

1/2 teaspoon ground cumin

1 clove garlic, finely minced

Salt and freshly ground black pepper

In Dutch oven, heat olive oil over medium-high heat until hot. Add
potatoes and onions; cook and stir 5 minutes. Add beef broth, green beans
and carrots. Bring mixture to a boil. Cover; reduce heat to low and simmer
10 minutes, stirring occasionally. Add spinach, bell pepper, parsley, basil,
cumin and garlic. Cover; simmer an additional 15 to 20 minutes or until
potatoes are tender. Season to taste with salt and black pepper. Serve hot.

Makes 6 to 8 servings

Vegetable Soup

Beef and Parsnip Stew

1¼ pounds beef stew meat, cut into ¾-inch cubes

½ cup all-purpose flour

2 tablespoons vegetable oil

4½ cups Beef Stock (recipe follows) or canned beef broth

½ cup dry red wine

1 teaspoon salt

½ teaspoon dried Italian seasoning

⅛ teaspoon black pepper

8 ounces peeled baby carrots

2 parsnips, peeled and cut into ⅜-inch slices

¾ cup sugar snap peas

1. Toss beef in flour to coat. Heat oil in large saucepan over medium-high heat. Add beef and coating flour; brown, stirring frequently.

2. Stir in Beef Stock, wine, salt, Italian seasoning and pepper. Bring to a boil over high heat. Reduce heat to medium-low; simmer, uncovered, 1 hour.

3. Add carrots. Cook 15 minutes. Add parsnips. Simmer 8 minutes or until vegetables and meat are tender.

4. Stir in peas. Cook and stir over medium heat until heated through.

Makes 5 servings

Parsnips are ivory-colored root vegetables very similar to carrots. They have a nutty, sweet flavor.

Beef Stock

4 pounds meaty beef bones
2 large onions, cut into wedges
2 large carrots, halved
4 ribs celery, halved
3½ quarts cold water, divided
8 sprigs parsley
2 bay leaves
1 teaspoon dried thyme leaves
6 black peppercorns
3 whole cloves

1. Preheat oven to 450°F. Rinse bones in cold water; arrange in large roasting pan. Place bones in large baking pan; roast in oven 30 minutes, turning once. Arrange onions, carrots and celery over bones. Roast 30 minutes more. Transfer bones and vegetables to stockpot or 5-quart Dutch oven. Skim fat from roasting pan and discard.

2. To deglaze pan, add 2 cups water to pan. Cook over medium-high heat, scraping up brown bits and stirring constantly 2 to 3 minutes or until mixture has reduced by about half. Add mixture to stockpot.

3. Add remaining 3 quarts water, parsley, bay leaves, thyme, peppercorns and cloves to stockpot. Bring to a boil over high heat. Reduce heat to medium-low; simmer, uncovered, 3 to 4 hours, skimming foam off top.

4. Remove stock from heat and cool slightly. Remove large bones. Strain stock through large sieve or colander lined with several layers of damp cheesecloth, discarding bones and vegetables.

5. Use immediately or refrigerate stock in tightly covered container up to 2 days or freeze stock in storage containers for several months.

Makes about 1½ quarts stock

Country Casseroles

Casseroles were one of Grandma's specialties. She could take the simplest ingredients and turn them into a great-tasting home-cooked meal—and now you can too with these easy recipes.

Biscuit-Topped Hearty Steak Pie

1^1/2 pounds top round steak, cooked and cut into 1-inch cubes

1 package (9 ounces) frozen baby carrots

1 package (9 ounces) frozen peas and pearl onions

1 large baking potato, cooked and cut into ^{1}/2-inch pieces

1 jar (18 ounces) home-style brown gravy

^{1}/2 teaspoon dried thyme leaves

^{1}/2 teaspoon black pepper

1 can (10 ounces) refrigerated flaky buttermilk biscuits

Preheat oven to 375°F. Spray 2-quart casserole with nonstick cooking spray.

Combine steak, frozen vegetables and potato in prepared dish. Stir in gravy, thyme and pepper.

Bake, uncovered, 40 minutes. Remove from oven. *Increase oven temperature to 400°F.* Top with biscuits and bake 8 to 10 minutes or until biscuits are golden brown.   *Makes 6 servings*

Choose your favorite vegetable combination, such as broccoli, cauliflower and carrots or corn and red peppers, as a substitute for the peas and carrots.

Apple, Bean and Ham Casserole

1 pound boneless ham

3 cans (15 ounces each) Great Northern beans, drained and
    rinsed

1 small onion, diced

1 medium Granny Smith apple, diced

3 tablespoons dark molasses

3 tablespoons packed brown sugar

1 tablespoon Dijon mustard

1 teaspoon ground allspice

$1/4$ cup thinly sliced green onions *or* 1 tablespoon chopped fresh
    parsley

1. Preheat oven to 350°F. Cut ham into 1-inch cubes. Combine ham, beans, onion, apple, molasses, brown sugar, mustard and allspice in 3-quart casserole; mix well. Cover; bake 45 minutes or until most liquid is absorbed. Cool casserole completely. Cover and refrigerate up to 2 days.

2. To complete recipe, stir $1/3$ cup water into casserole. Microwave at HIGH 10 minutes or until hot and bubbly. Or, heat in preheated 350°F oven 40 minutes or until hot and bubbly. Sprinkle with green onions before serving. *Makes 6 servings*

*Allspice was given its name because it tastes like a
mixture of cinnamon, nutmeg and cloves.*

Apple, Bean and Ham Casserole

Pepperidge Farm® Turkey & Stuffing Bake

1 can (14^1/$_2$ ounces) SWANSON® Chicken Broth (1^3/$_4$ cups)
   Generous dash pepper
1 stalk celery, chopped (about ^{1}/$_2$ cup)
1 small onion, coarsely chopped (about ^{1}/$_4$ cup)
4 cups PEPPERIDGE FARM® Herb Seasoned Stuffing
4 servings sliced roasted *or* deli turkey (about 12 ounces)
1 jar (12 ounces) FRANCO-AMERICAN® Slow Roast™ Turkey
   Gravy

1. In medium saucepan mix broth, pepper, celery and onion. Over high heat, heat to a boil. Reduce heat to low. Cover and cook 5 minutes or until vegetables are tender. Add stuffing. Mix lightly.

2. Spoon into 2-quart shallow baking dish. Arrange turkey over stuffing. Pour gravy over turkey.

3. Bake at 350°F. for 30 minutes or until hot.   *Makes 4 servings*

Prep Time: 15 minutes
Cook Time: 30 minutes

Family Favorite Hamburger Casserole

1 tablespoon CRISCO® Vegetable Oil plus additional for oiling
1 cup chopped onion
1 pound ground beef round
1 package (9 ounces) frozen cut green beans
3 cups frozen southern style hash brown potatoes
1 can ($10^3/_4$ ounces) zesty tomato soup
$1/_2$ cup water
1 teaspoon dried basil leaves
$3/_4$ teaspoon salt
$1/_4$ teaspoon pepper
$1/_4$ cup plain dry bread crumbs

1. Heat oven to 350°F. Oil $11^3/_4 \times 7^1/_2 \times 2$-inch baking dish lightly.

2. Heat Crisco Oil in large skillet on medium-high heat. Add onion. Cook and stir until tender. Add meat. Cook until browned, stirring occasionally. Add beans. Cook and stir 5 minutes or until thawed. Add potatoes.

3. Combine tomato soup and water in small bowl. Stir until well blended. Stir into skillet. Stir in basil, salt and pepper. Spoon into baking dish. Sprinkle with bread crumbs.

4. Bake at 350°F for 30 minutes or until potatoes are tender. Let stand 5 minutes before serving. *Makes 4 servings*

Country Chicken Pot Pie

   2 tablespoons margarine or butter

$^3/_4$ pound boneless skinless chicken breasts, cut into 1-inch pieces

$^3/_4$ teaspoon salt

   8 ounces fresh green beans, cut into 1-inch pieces (2 cups)

$^1/_2$ cup chopped red bell pepper

$^1/_2$ cup thinly sliced celery

   3 tablespoons all-purpose flour

$^1/_2$ cup chicken broth

$^1/_2$ cup half-and-half

   1 teaspoon dried thyme leaves

$^1/_2$ teaspoon rubbed sage

   1 cup frozen pearl onions

$^1/_2$ cup frozen corn

      Pastry for single-crust 10-inch pie

Preheat oven to 425°F. Spray 10-inch deep-dish pie plate with nonstick cooking spray.

Melt margarine in large deep skillet over medium-high heat. Add chicken; cook and stir 3 minutes or until no longer pink in centers. Sprinkle with salt. Add beans, pepper and celery; cook and stir 3 minutes.

Sprinkle flour evenly over chicken and vegetables; cook and stir 1 minute. Stir in broth, half-and-half, thyme and sage; bring to a boil over high heat. Reduce heat to low and simmer 3 minutes or until sauce is very thick. Stir in onions and corn. Return to a simmer; cook and stir 1 minute.

Transfer mixture to prepared pie plate. Place pie crust over chicken mixture; turn edge under and crimp to seal. Cut 4 slits in pie crust to allow steam to escape.

Bake 20 minutes or until crust is light golden brown and mixture is hot and bubbly. Let stand 5 minutes before serving. *Makes 6 servings*

Country Chicken Pot Pie

Ham & Macaroni Twists

2 cups rotini or elbow macaroni, cooked in unsalted water and
   drained
1 1/2 cups (8 ounces) cubed cooked ham
1 1/3 cups FRENCH'S® French Fried Onions, divided
1 package (10 ounces) frozen broccoli spears,* thawed and drained
1 cup milk
1 can (10 3/4 ounces) condensed cream of celery soup
1 cup (4 ounces) shredded Cheddar cheese, divided
1/4 teaspoon garlic powder
1/4 teaspoon pepper

*1 small head fresh broccoli (about 1/2 pound) may be substituted for frozen spears. Divide into spears and cook 3 to 4 minutes before using.

Preheat oven to 350°F. In 12×8-inch baking dish, combine hot macaroni, ham and 2/3 cup French Fried Onions. Divide broccoli spears into 6 small bunches. Arrange bunches of spears down center of dish, alternating direction of flowerets. In small bowl, combine milk, soup, 1/2 cup cheese and the seasonings; pour over casserole. Bake, covered, at 350°F for 30 minutes or until heated through. Top with remaining cheese and sprinkle remaining 2/3 cup onions down center; bake, uncovered, 5 minutes or until onions are golden brown.

Makes 4 to 6 servings

Microwave Directions: In 12×8-inch microwave-safe dish, prepare macaroni mixture and arrange broccoli spears as above. Prepare soup mixture as above; pour over casserole. Cook, covered, on HIGH 8 minutes or until broccoli is done. Rotate dish halfway through cooking time. Top with remaining cheese and onions as above; cook, uncovered, 1 minute or until cheese melts. Let stand 5 minutes.

Main-Dish Pie

    1 package (8 rolls) refrigerated crescent rolls
    1 pound lean ground beef
    1 medium onion, chopped
    1 can (12 ounces) beef or mushroom gravy
    1 box (10 ounces) BIRDS EYE® frozen Green Peas, thawed
$^1/_2$ cup shredded Swiss cheese
    6 slices tomato

• Preheat oven to 350°F.

• Unroll dough and separate rolls. Spread to cover bottom of ungreased 9-inch pie pan. Press together to form lower crust. Bake 10 minutes.

• Meanwhile, in large skillet, brown beef and onion; drain excess fat.

• Stir in gravy and peas; cook until heated through.

• Pour mixture into partially baked crust. Sprinkle with cheese.

• Bake 10 to 15 minutes or until crust is brown and cheese is melted.

• Arrange tomato slices over pie; bake 2 minutes more.

Makes 6 servings

Prep Time: 10 minutes
Cook Time: 20 to 25 minutes

Mexicali Cornbread Casserole

Mexicali Cornbread Casserole

2^{1}/$_{2}$ cups frozen mixed vegetables, thawed

1^{1}/$_{2}$ cups cubed HILLSHIRE FARM® Ham

1 package (10 ounces) cornbread stuffing mix

2 cups milk

3 eggs, lightly beaten

Salt and black pepper to taste

^{1}/$_{2}$ cup (2 ounces) shredded taco-flavored cheese

Preheat oven to 375°F.

Combine mixed vegetables, Ham and stuffing mix in small casserole; set aside. Combine milk, eggs, salt and pepper in medium bowl; pour over ham mixture. Bake, covered, 45 minutes. Top with cheese; bake, uncovered, 3 minutes or until cheese is melted.   *Makes 4 servings*

Prego® Baked Ziti Supreme

    1 pound ground beef
    1 medium onion, chopped (about $^1/_2$ cup)
    1 jar (28 ounces) PREGO® Pasta Sauce with Fresh Mushrooms
 1 $^1/_2$ cups shredded mozzarella cheese (6 ounces)
    5 cups hot cooked medium tube-shaped macaroni (about 3 cups
       uncooked)
 $^1/_4$ cup grated Parmesan cheese

1. In large saucepan over medium-high heat, cook beef and onion until beef is browned, stirring to separate meat. Pour off fat.

2. Stir in pasta sauce, *1 cup* mozzarella cheese and macaroni. Spoon into 3-quart shallow baking dish. Sprinkle with remaining mozzarella cheese and Parmesan cheese. Bake at 350°F. for 30 minutes.

Makes 6 servings

Prep Time: 25 minutes
Cook Time: 30 minutes

A salad of mixed greens and hot toasted garlic bread
team perfectly with this quick and easy casserole.

49

Savory Pork Chop Supper

6 medium potatoes, thinly sliced (about 5 cups)

1 1/3 cups FRENCH'S® French Fried Onions, divided

1 jar (2 ounces) sliced mushrooms, drained

2 tablespoons butter or margarine

1/4 cup soy sauce

1 1/2 teaspoons ground mustard

1/2 teaspoon FRANK'S® REDHOT® Hot Sauce

1/8 teaspoon garlic powder

1 tablespoon vegetable oil

6 pork chops, 1/2 to 3/4 inch thick

Preheat oven to 350°F. In 12×8-inch baking dish, layer half the potatoes and 2/3 cup French Fried Onions. Top with mushrooms and remaining potatoes. In small saucepan, melt butter; stir in soy sauce, mustard, REDHOT sauce and garlic powder. Brush half the soy sauce mixture over potatoes. In large skillet, heat oil. Brown pork chops on both sides; drain. Arrange chops over potatoes and brush with remaining soy sauce mixture. Bake, covered, at 350°F for 1 hour. Bake, uncovered, 15 minutes or until pork chops and potatoes are done. Top chops with remaining 2/3 cup onions; bake, uncovered, 5 minutes or until onions are golden brown.   *Makes 4 to 6 servings*

Mustard Chicken & Vegetables

$^1/_4$ cup FRENCH'S® Dijon or Classic Yellow® Mustard

$^1/_4$ cup vegetable oil

1 tablespoon red wine vinegar

$^1/_2$ teaspoon dried oregano, crumbled

$^1/_4$ teaspoon pepper

$^1/_4$ teaspoon salt

2 pounds chicken pieces, fat trimmed

2 cups (8 ounces) fusilli or rotini, cooked in unsalted water and drained

1 can ($10^3/_4$ ounces) condensed cream of chicken soup

1 cup each zucchini and yellow squash, cut into 1-inch chunks

$^1/_2$ cup milk

$1^1/_3$ cups FRENCH'S® French Fried Onions, divided

1 medium tomato, cut into wedges

Preheat oven to 375°F. In large bowl, combine mustard, oil, vinegar and seasonings; mix well. Toss chicken in mustard sauce until coated. Reserve remaining mustard sauce. Arrange chicken in 13×9-inch baking dish. Bake, uncovered, at 375°F for 30 minutes. Stir hot pasta, soup, squash, milk and $^2/_3$ cup French Fried Onions into remaining mustard sauce. Spoon pasta mixture into baking dish, placing it under and around chicken. Bake, uncovered, 15 to 20 minutes or until chicken is done. Top pasta mixture with tomato wedges and top chicken with remaining $^2/_3$ cup onions; bake, uncovered, 3 minutes or until onions are golden brown.

Makes 4 to 6 servings

Shepherd's Pie

1 1/3 cups instant mashed potato buds

1 2/3 cups milk

2 tablespoons margarine or butter

1 teaspoon salt, divided

1 pound ground beef

1/4 teaspoon black pepper

1 jar (12 ounces) beef gravy

1 package (10 ounces) frozen mixed vegetables, thawed and drained

3/4 cup grated Parmesan cheese

1. Preheat broiler. Prepare 4 servings of mashed potatoes according to package directions using milk, margarine and 1/2 teaspoon salt.

2. While mashed potatoes are cooking, brown meat in medium broilerproof skillet over medium-high heat, stirring to separate meat. Drain drippings. Sprinkle meat with remaining 1/2 teaspoon salt and pepper. Add gravy and vegetables; mix well. Cook over medium-low heat 5 minutes or until hot.

3. Spoon prepared potatoes around outside edge of skillet, leaving 3-inch circle in center. Sprinkle cheese evenly over potatoes. Broil 4 to 5 inches from heat source 3 minutes or until cheese is golden brown and meat mixture is bubbly.   *Makes 4 servings*

Prep and Cook Time: 28 minutes

Shepherd's Pie

Oven Chicken & Rice

  1 can (10³/₄ ounces) condensed cream of mushroom soup
1¹/₃ cups water
  1 cup long-grain or converted rice
  1 teaspoon dried dill weed, divided
¹/₄ teaspoon black pepper
  1 chicken (3 pounds), cut up and skinned
¹/₂ cup crushed multi-grain crackers
  1 teaspoon paprika
  2 tablespoons butter or margarine, melted
    Fresh dill sprigs for garnish

Preheat oven to 375°F. Combine soup, water, rice, ³/₄ teaspoon dill weed and pepper in 13×9-inch baking dish. Arrange chicken pieces on top of rice mixture. Cover tightly with foil. Bake 45 minutes.

Sprinkle chicken pieces with crackers, paprika and remaining ¹/₄ teaspoon dill. Drizzle with butter. Bake 5 to 10 minutes or until chicken is tender. Season to taste with salt and pepper. Garnish with dill sprig, if desired.

Makes 4 to 5 servings

Long-grain rice grains are 3 to 4 times as long as
they are wide. The cooked grains remain separate,
light and fluffy.

Oven Chicken & Rice

Traditional Sunday Suppers

Sunday supper at Grandma's was always so delicious! The whole family was there, but she knew just how to make you feel special—by making your favorite dish!

Harvest Pot Roast with Sweet Potatoes

    1 envelope LIPTON® RECIPE SECRETS® Onion Soup Mix
1 1/2 cups water
  1/4 cup soy sauce
    2 tablespoons firmly packed dark brown sugar
    1 teaspoon ground ginger (optional)
    1 (3- to 3 1/2-pound) boneless pot roast (rump, chuck or round)
    4 large sweet potatoes, peeled, if desired, and cut into large chunks
    3 tablespoons water
    2 tablespoons all-purpose flour

1. Preheat oven to 325°F. In Dutch oven or 5-quart heavy ovenproof saucepot, combine soup mix, water, soy sauce, brown sugar and ginger; add roast.

2. Cover and bake 1 hour 45 minutes.

3. Add potatoes and bake covered an additional 45 minutes or until beef and potatoes are tender.

4. Remove roast and potatoes to serving platter and keep warm; reserve juices.

5. In small cup, with wire whisk, blend water and flour. In Dutch oven, add flour mixture to reserved juices. Bring to a boil over high heat. Boil, stirring occasionally, 2 minutes. Serve with roast and potatoes.

Makes 6 servings

Chicken in Mushroom Sauce

2 cups uncooked instant white rice

2 tablespoons olive oil

4 boneless skinless chicken breast halves (1 pound)

1 cup sliced mushrooms

1 small onion, thinly sliced

1 teaspoon bottled minced garlic

1 can (10¾ ounces) cream of mushroom soup

1. Cook rice according to package directions.

2. While rice is cooking, heat oil in large nonstick skillet over medium heat. Cook chicken breasts 3 to 4 minutes per side or until lightly browned. Remove chicken; set aside.

3. Add mushrooms, onion and garlic to skillet. Cook 1 minute, stirring constantly. Reduce heat to low; stir in soup and black pepper to taste. Add chicken and cook about 7 minutes or until chicken is no longer pink in center. Serve over rice. *Makes 4 servings*

Prep and Cook Time: 25 minutes

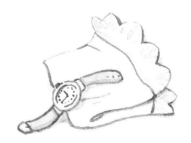

Chicken in Mushroom Sauce

Easy Cheesy Lasagna

2 tablespoons olive oil

3 small zucchini, quartered and thinly sliced

1 package (8 ounces) mushrooms, thinly sliced

1 medium onion, chopped

5 cloves garlic, minced

2 containers (15 ounces each) reduced-fat ricotta cheese

$^{1}/_{4}$ cup grated Parmesan cheese

2 eggs

$^{1}/_{2}$ teaspoon dried Italian seasoning

$^{1}/_{4}$ teaspoon garlic salt

$^{1}/_{8}$ teaspoon black pepper

1 can (28 ounces) crushed tomatoes in purée, undrained

1 jar (26 ounces) spaghetti sauce

1 package (16 ounces) lasagna noodles, uncooked

4 cups (16 ounces) shredded mozzarella cheese, divided

Preheat oven to 375°F. Spray 13×9-inch baking dish or lasagna pan with nonstick cooking spray.

Heat oil in large skillet over medium heat until hot. Add zucchini, mushrooms, onion and garlic. Cook and stir 5 minutes or until vegetables are tender. Set aside.

Combine ricotta, Parmesan, eggs, Italian seasoning, garlic salt and pepper in medium bowl. Combine tomatoes and spaghetti sauce in another medium bowl.

Easy Cheesy Lasagna

Spread about ³/₄ cup tomato mixture in prepared dish. Place layer of noodles over tomato mixture, overlapping noodles. Spread half of vegetable mixture over noodles; top with half of ricotta mixture. Sprinkle 1 cup mozzarella over ricotta mixture. Place second layer of noodles over mozzarella. Spread about 1 cup tomato mixture over noodles. Top with remaining vegetable and ricotta cheese mixtures. Sprinkle 1 cup mozzarella over ricotta mixture. Place third layer of noodles over mozzarella. Spread remaining tomato mixture over noodles. Sprinkle remaining 2 cups mozzarella evenly over top.

Cover tightly with foil and bake 1 hour or until noodles in center are soft. Uncover; bake 5 minutes or until cheese is melted and lightly browned. Remove from oven; cover and let stand 15 minutes before serving.

Makes 6 servings

Honey Glazed Ham

2 (8-ounce) fully-cooked ham steaks

$^1/_4$ cup honey

3 tablespoons water

1$^1/_2$ teaspoons dry mustard

$^1/_2$ teaspoon ground ginger

$^1/_4$ teaspoon ground cloves

Pan-fry or broil ham steaks until lightly browned and thoroughly heated. Remove ham from skillet or broiler pan. Combine honey, water and spices; add to pan drippings and bring to a boil. Simmer 1 to 2 minutes. Brush over ham. Serve ham with remaining sauce. *Makes 4 servings*

Favorite recipe from **National Honey Board**

Honey is one of the only foods that will never go bad, no matter how long you keep it. If honey has crystallized, soften it in the microwave. Place the jar, without the lid, in the microwave and heat at HIGH about 30 seconds. Stir and let stand 1 minute.

Leg of Lamb with Apricot Stuffing

1 (6-ounce) package dried apricots, snipped

$^1/_4$ cup apple juice

$^1/_4$ cup wild rice, rinsed and drained

1$^1/_2$ cups chicken broth

$^1/_2$ cup long-grain rice

$^1/_4$ cup chutney

$^1/_4$ cup sliced green onions

2 teaspoons dried basil leaves

$^1/_2$ teaspoon lemon pepper

3 to 3$^1/_2$ pounds American leg of lamb, shank half, boned and butterflied

$^1/_4$ teaspoon salt

$^1/_4$ teaspoon ground black pepper

In bowl, combine apricots and apple juice; cover and let stand 20 minutes, stirring occasionally. In saucepan, combine wild rice and broth. Bring to a boil; reduce heat. Cover and simmer 40 minutes. Add long-grain rice. Cover and simmer 15 minutes more. Remove from heat. Let stand, covered, 5 minutes. Stir in apricot mixture, chutney (cut up any large chutney pieces), green onions, basil and lemon pepper.

Trim any fat from lamb. With boned side up, pound meat with meat mallet to even thickness, about 4 inches by 20 inches. Sprinkle lightly with salt and pepper. Spread rice mixture over meat. Roll up, starting with narrow end; tie securely. Place roast on end, spiral side up, on rack in shallow roasting pan. Cover exposed rice mixture with small piece of foil. Roast at 325°F for 1$^3/_4$ hours, or to medium doneness (150° to 160°F). Remove from oven. Let stand about 10 minutes. Remove strings; cut into wedges to serve. *Makes 12 servings*

Favorite recipe from **American Lamb Council**

Pepper Steak

1 tablespoon coarsely cracked black pepper

$^1/_2$ teaspoon dried rosemary

2 beef filet mignons or rib-eye steaks, 1 inch thick (4 to 6 ounces each)

1 tablespoon butter or margarine

1 tablespoon vegetable oil

$^1/_4$ cup brandy or dry red wine

1. Combine pepper and rosemary in bowl. Coat both sides of steaks with mixture.

2. Heat butter and oil in large skillet until hot; add steaks and cook over medium to medium-high heat 5 to 7 minutes per side for medium, or to desired degree of doneness. Remove steaks from skillet. Sprinkle lightly with salt and cover to keep warm.

3. Add brandy to skillet; bring to a boil over high heat, scraping particles from bottom of skillet. Boil about 1 minute or until liquid is reduced by half. Spoon sauce over steaks.   *Makes 2 servings*

Prep and Cook Time: 17 minutes

Pepper Steak

Lemon-Dijon Chicken with Potatoes

2 lemons

$^1/_2$ cup chopped fresh parsley

2 tablespoons Dijon mustard

4 cloves garlic, minced

2 teaspoons extra-virgin olive oil

1 teaspoon dried rosemary leaves

$^3/_4$ teaspoon black pepper

$^1/_2$ teaspoon salt

1 whole chicken (about $3^1/_2$ pounds)

$1^1/_2$ pounds small red potatoes, cut into halves

Preheat oven 350°F. Squeeze 3 tablespoons juice from lemons; reserve squeezed lemon halves. Combine parsley, lemon juice, mustard, garlic, oil, rosemary, pepper and salt in small bowl; blend well. Reserve 2 tablespoons mixture.

Place chicken on rack in baking pan; gently slide fingers between skin and meat of chicken breasts and drumsticks to separate skin from the meat, being careful not to tear skin. Spoon remaining parsley mixture between skin and meat (secure breast skin with wooden picks, if necessary) and place lemon halves in cavity of chicken. Bake 30 minutes.

Meanwhile, toss potatoes with reserved parsley mixture until coated. Arrange potatoes around chicken; bake 1 hour or until juices in chicken run clear and thermometer inserted in thickest part of thigh registers 180°F. Let chicken stand 10 minutes before removing skin and slicing. Sprinkle any accumulated parsley mixture over chicken and potatoes.

Makes 6 servings

Maple-Cranberry Pork Chops

4 well-trimmed center cut pork chops ($^{1}/_{2}$ inch thick)

1 cup dry red wine or apple juice

$^{1}/_{2}$ cup maple syrup or maple-flavored syrup

$^{1}/_{2}$ cup dried cranberries

1 tablespoon cold water

2 teaspoons cornstarch

1. Spray large nonstick skillet with nonstick cooking spray. Heat skillet over medium-high heat until hot. Add pork chops; cook 3 to 5 minutes per side or just until browned and pork is no longer pink in center. Remove from skillet; keep warm.

2. Add wine, syrup and cranberries to skillet; cook and stir over medium-high heat 2 to 3 minutes.

3. Combine water and cornstarch in small bowl; stir until smooth. Add cornstarch mixture to skillet; cook and stir about 1 minute or until thickened and clear. Reduce heat to medium. Return pork chops to skillet; spoon sauce over and simmer 1 minute. *Makes 4 servings*

Prep and Cook Time: 20 minutes

Southern Fried Catfish with Hush Puppies

Southern Fried Catfish with Hush Puppies

Hush Puppy Batter (recipe follows)
4 catfish fillets (about 1 1/2 pounds)
1/2 cup yellow cornmeal
3 tablespoons all-purpose flour
1 1/2 teaspoons salt
1/4 teaspoon ground red pepper
Vegetable oil for frying
Fresh parsley sprigs for garnish

Prepare Hush Puppy Batter; set aside.

Rinse catfish and pat dry with paper towels. Combine cornmeal, flour, salt and red pepper in shallow dish. Dip fish in cornmeal mixture. Heat 1 inch of oil in large, heavy saucepan over medium heat until oil registers 375°F on deep-fry thermometer.

Fry fish, a few pieces at a time, 4 to 5 minutes or until golden brown and fish flakes easily when tested with fork. Adjust heat to maintain temperature. (Allow temperature of oil to return to 375°F between each batch.) Drain fish on paper towels.

To make Hush Puppies, drop batter by tablespoonfuls into hot oil. Fry, a few pieces at a time, 2 minutes or until golden brown. Garnish, if desired.

Makes 4 servings

Hush Puppy Batter

1 1/2 cups yellow cornmeal

1/2 cup all-purpose flour

2 teaspoons baking powder

1/2 teaspoon salt

1 cup milk

1 small onion, minced

1 egg, slightly beaten

Combine cornmeal, flour, baking powder and salt in medium bowl. Add milk, onion and egg. Stir until well combined. Allow batter to stand 5 to 10 minutes before frying. *Makes about 24 hush puppies*

Chicken Vesuvio

1 whole chicken (about 3¾ pounds)
¼ cup olive oil
3 tablespoons lemon juice
4 cloves garlic, minced
3 large baking potatoes, peeled and cut into quarters lengthwise
Salt and lemon pepper

Preheat oven to 375°F. Place chicken, breast side down, on rack in large shallow roasting pan. Combine oil, lemon juice and garlic in small bowl; brush over chicken. Set aside remaining oil mixture. Roast chicken 30 minutes.

Turn chicken breast side up. Add potatoes to roasting pan. Brush chicken and potatoes with remaining oil mixture; sprinkle with salt and lemon pepper to taste. Roast chicken and potatoes, basting occasionally with pan juices, 50 minutes or until meat thermometer inserted into thickest part of chicken thigh, not touching bone, registers 180°F and potatoes are tender.   *Makes 4 to 6 servings*

Chicken Vesuvio

Campbell's® Best Ever Meatloaf

1 can (10³/4 ounces) CAMPBELL'S® Condensed Tomato Soup
2 pounds ground beef
1 pouch CAMPBELL'S® Dry Onion Soup and Recipe Mix
¹/2 cup dry bread crumbs
1 egg, beaten
¹/4 cup water

1. Mix *¹/2 cup* tomato soup, beef, onion soup mix, bread crumbs and egg *thoroughly.* In baking pan shape *firmly* into 8- by 4-inch loaf.

2. Bake at 350°F. for 1¹/4 hours or until meat loaf is no longer pink (160°F.).

3. In small saucepan mix *2 tablespoons* drippings, remaining tomato soup and water. Heat through. Serve with meat loaf.   *Makes 8 servings*

Prep Time: 10 minutes
Cook Time: 1 hour 20 minutes

To meet USDA standards, all ground beef must be at least 70 percent lean. Ground sirloin and ground round are the leanest. Ground chuck contains more fat and therefore produces juicier hamburgers and meatloaf.

Campbell's® Best Ever Meatloaf

All the Trimmings

Family dinners just wouldn't be complete without the scrumptious sides that Grandma used to serve. Sometimes they were so good they became the center of attention at the table!

Chutney'd Squash Circles

   2 acorn squash (1 pound each)
   2 tablespoons butter or margarine
   $^1/_2$ cup prepared chutney
   2 tablespoons water
      Purple kale and scented geranium leaves for garnish*

*Use only non-toxic leaves.

1. Preheat oven to 400°F. Slice tip and stem end from squash. Scoop out and discard seeds. Cut squash crosswise into $^3/_4$-inch rings.

2. Tear off 18-inch square of heavy aluminum foil. Center foil in 13×9-inch baking dish. Dot foil with butter and place squash on butter, slightly overlapping rings. Spoon chutney over slices and sprinkle with water.

3. Bring foil on long sides of pan together in center, folding over to make tight seam. Crimp ends to form tight seal.

4. Bake 20 to 30 minutes until squash is fork-tender. Transfer to warm serving plate. Pour pan drippings over squash. Garnish, if desired.

Makes 4 side-dish servings

Garlic Mashed Potatoes

6 medium all-purpose potatoes, peeled, if desired, and cut into
chunks (about 3 pounds)

Water

1 envelope LIPTON® RECIPE SECRETS® Garlic Mushroom
Soup Mix*

$^1/_2$ cup milk

$^1/_2$ cup margarine or butter, softened

*Also terrific with LIPTON® RECIPE SECRETS® Savory Herb with Garlic, Onion or
Golden Onion Soup Mix.*

1. In 4-quart saucepan, cover potatoes with water; bring to a boil.

2. Reduce heat to low and simmer uncovered 20 minutes or until potatoes
are very tender; drain.

3. Return potatoes to saucepan, then mash. Stir in remaining ingredients.

Makes 8 servings

*Potatoes, especially with the skins, are good sources
of vitamin C, phosphorous and potassium.*

Garlic Mashed Potatoes

Carrots with Raisin Sauce

2 bags (16 ounces each) BIRDS EYE® frozen Sliced Carrots

$^1/_4$ cup brown sugar

1 tablespoon cornstarch

$^2/_3$ cup water

$^1/_2$ cup raisins

2 teaspoons cider vinegar

• Cook carrots according to package directions.

• Blend brown sugar and cornstarch in small saucepan.

• Add remaining ingredients; cook over low heat until sauce is thickened and raisins are plump.

• Toss carrots with sauce.   *Makes about 8 servings*

Prep Time: 2 to 3 minutes
Cook Time: 8 to 10 minutes

Campbell's® Creamed Onion Bake

4 tablespoons margarine *or* butter

1¹/₂ cups PEPPERIDGE FARM® Corn Bread Stuffing

2 tablespoons chopped fresh parsley *or* 2 teaspoons dried parsley flakes

3 large onions, cut in half and sliced (about 3 cups)

1 can (10³/₄ ounces) CAMPBELL'S® Condensed Cream of Mushroom Soup *or* 98% Fat Free Cream of Mushroom Soup

¹/₄ cup milk

1 cup frozen peas

1 cup shredded Cheddar cheese (4 ounces)

1. Melt *2 tablespoons* margarine and mix with stuffing and parsley. Set aside.

2. In medium skillet over medium heat, heat remaining margarine. Add onions and cook until tender.

3. Stir in soup, milk and peas. Spoon into 2-quart shallow baking dish. Sprinkle cheese and stuffing mixture over soup mixture.

4. Bake at 350°F. for 30 minutes or until hot.   *Makes 6 servings*

Prep Time: 15 minutes

Cook Time: 30 minutes

Broccoli Casserole with Crumb Topping

2 slices day-old white bread, coarsely crumbled (about 1¼ cups)
½ cup shredded mozzarella cheese (about 2 ounces)
2 tablespoons chopped fresh parsley (optional)
2 tablespoons olive or vegetable oil
1 clove garlic, finely chopped
6 cups broccoli florets and/or cauliflowerets
1 envelope LIPTON® RECIPE SECRETS® Onion Soup Mix*
1 cup water
1 large tomato, chopped

*Also terrific with LIPTON® RECIPE SECRETS® Garlic Mushroom Soup Mix.

1. In small bowl, combine bread crumbs, cheese, parsley, 1 tablespoon oil and garlic; set aside.

2. In 12-inch skillet, heat remaining 1 tablespoon oil over medium heat and cook broccoli, stirring frequently, 2 minutes.

3. Stir in soup mix blended with water. Bring to a boil over high heat. Reduce heat to low and simmer uncovered, stirring occasionally, 8 minutes or until broccoli is almost tender. Add tomato and simmer 2 minutes.

4. Spoon vegetable mixture into 1½-quart casserole; top with bread crumb mixture. Broil 1½ minutes or until crumbs are golden and cheese is melted. *Makes 6 servings*

Broccoli Casserole with Crumb Topping

Pepperidge Farm® Vegetable Stuffing Bake

4 cups PEPPERIDGE FARM® Herb Seasoned Stuffing

2 tablespoons margarine *or* butter, melted

1 can (10³/₄ ounces) CAMPBELL'S® Condensed Cream of
    Mushroom Soup *or* 98% Fat Free Cream of Mushroom Soup

¹/₂ cup sour cream

2 small zucchini, shredded (about 2 cups)

2 medium carrots, shredded (about 1 cup)

1 small onion, finely chopped (about ¹/₄ cup)

1. Mix *1 cup* stuffing and margarine. Set aside.

2. Mix soup, sour cream, zucchini, carrots and onion. Add remaining stuffing. Mix lightly. Spoon into 1¹/₂-quart casserole. Sprinkle with reserved stuffing mixture.

3. Bake at 350°F. for 35 minutes or until hot.   *Makes 6 servings*

Prep Time: 15 minutes
Cook Time: 35 minutes

*It may sound Italian, but zucchini is actually an
American summer squash that traveled abroad and
then returned.*

Sweet Potato Puffs

    2 pounds sweet potatoes

$^1/_3$ cup orange juice

    1 egg, beaten

    1 tablespoon grated orange peel

$^1/_2$ teaspoon ground nutmeg

$^1/_4$ cup chopped pecans

1. Peel and cut sweet potatoes into 1-inch pieces. Place potatoes in medium saucepan. Add enough water to cover; bring to a boil over medium-high heat. Cook 10 to 15 minutes or until tender. Drain potatoes and place in large bowl; mash until smooth. Add orange juice, egg, orange peel and nutmeg; mix well.

2. Preheat oven to 375°F. Spray baking sheet with nonstick cooking spray. Spoon potato mixture into 10 mounds on prepared baking sheet. Sprinkle pecans on tops of mounds.

3. Bake 30 minutes or until centers are hot. Garnish, if desired.

Makes 10 servings

Savory Lentil Casserole

$1^{1}/_{4}$ cups uncooked dried brown or green lentils, rinsed and sorted

2 tablespoons olive oil

1 large onion, chopped

3 cloves garlic, minced

8 ounces fresh shiitake or button mushrooms, sliced

2 tablespoons all-purpose flour

$1^{1}/_{2}$ cups beef broth

1 tablespoon Worcestershire sauce

1 tablespoon balsamic vinegar

4 ounces Canadian bacon, minced

$^{1}/_{2}$ teaspoon *each* salt and black pepper

$^{1}/_{2}$ cup grated Parmesan cheese

2 to 3 plum tomatoes, seeded and chopped

1. Preheat oven to 400°F. Place lentils in medium saucepan; cover with 1 inch water. Bring to a boil over high heat. Reduce heat to low. Simmer, covered, 20 to 25 minutes until lentils are barely tender; drain.

2. Meanwhile, heat oil in large skillet over medium heat. Add onion and garlic; cook and stir 10 minutes. Add mushrooms; cook and stir 10 minutes or until mushrooms are tender. Sprinkle flour over mushroom mixture. Cook and stir 1 minute. Stir in broth, Worcestershire, vinegar, bacon, salt and pepper. Cook and stir until mixture is thick and bubbly.

3. Grease $1^{1}/_{2}$-quart casserole. Stir lentils into mushroom mixture. Spread evenly into prepared casserole. Sprinkle with cheese. Bake 20 minutes.

4. Sprinkle tomatoes over casserole just before serving. Garnish with thyme and Italian parsley, if desired. *Makes 4 servings*

Savory Lentil Casserole

Broth-Braised Brussels Sprouts

1 pound fresh Brussels sprouts
$^1/_2$ cup condensed beef broth *or* $^1/_2$ cup water plus 2 teaspoons
    instant beef bouillon granules
1 tablespoon butter or margarine, softened
$^1/_4$ cup freshly grated Parmesan cheese
Paprika

1. Trim stems from Brussels sprouts and pull off outer discolored leaves.

2. Use large enough saucepan to allow sprouts to fit in single layer. Place sprouts and broth in saucepan. Bring to a boil; reduce heat. Cover; simmer about 5 minutes or just until sprouts turn bright green and are crisp-tender.

3. Uncover; simmer until liquid is almost evaporated. Toss cooked sprouts with butter, then cheese. Sprinkle with paprika to taste. Garnish as desired.

Makes 4 side-dish servings

Tip: For faster, more even cooking, cut an "X" deep into the stem end of each Brussels sprout.

86

Broth-Braised Brussels Sprouts

Herbed Cauliflower Casserole

5 cups cauliflower florets (about 1¼ pounds)

1 tablespoon margarine, melted

1 small red bell pepper, cored, seeded and quartered

2 tablespoons water

3 large tomatoes, peeled, seeded and coarsely chopped

2 to 3 teaspoons chopped fresh tarragon

½ teaspoon chopped fresh parsley

⅓ cup (about 9 to 10) coarsely crushed unsalted saltine crackers

1. Preheat oven to 450°F. Toss cauliflower with margarine in large bowl; place cauliflower and bell pepper, cut sides down, in one layer in shallow baking pan. Add water to pan. Roast vegetables 15 minutes; *reduce oven temperature to 425°F.* Continue roasting 25 to 28 minutes until cauliflower is tender and golden brown and bell pepper skin has blistered. Remove bell pepper pieces to plate and transfer cauliflower to 11×7-inch baking dish. *Reduce oven temperature to 400°F.*

2. Place tomatoes in food processor or blender. Remove and discard skin from bell pepper. Add bell pepper to food processor; process until smooth. Add tarragon and parsley; blend well.

3. Pour tomato sauce over cauliflower; bake 10 minutes or until cauliflower is hot and bubbly. Sprinkle with cracker crumbs just before serving. Garnish, if desired.   *Makes 5 (¾-cup) servings*

Herbed Cauliflower Casserole

Grandma's Cookie Jar

Going to Grandma's meant raiding her cookie jar. It was always brimming with home-baked treats. Fill your own cookie jar with the same tasty cookies and love, just like Grandma did.

Raspberry Pecan Thumbprints

   2 cups all-purpose flour

   1 cup pecan pieces, finely chopped and divided

$^1/_2$ teaspoon ground cinnamon

$^1/_4$ teaspoon ground allspice

$^1/_8$ teaspoon salt

   1 cup butter, softened

$^1/_2$ cup packed light brown sugar

   2 teaspoons vanilla

$^1/_3$ cup seedless raspberry jam

Preheat oven to 350°F. Combine flour, $^1/_2$ cup pecans, cinnamon, allspice and salt in medium bowl.

Beat butter in large bowl with electric mixer at medium speed until smooth. Gradually beat in sugar; increase speed to high and beat until light and fluffy. Beat in vanilla until blended. Beat in flour mixture at low speed just until blended.

Form dough into 1-inch balls; flatten slightly and place on ungreased cookie sheets. Press down with thumb in center of each ball to form indentation. Pinch together any cracks in dough.

Fill each indentation with generous $^1/_4$ teaspoon jam. Sprinkle filled cookies with remaining $^1/_2$ cup pecans.

Bake 14 minutes or until just set. Let cookies stand on cookie sheets 5 minutes; transfer to wire racks to cool completely. Store in airtight container at room temperature. Cookies are best day after baking.

Makes 36 cookies

Date-Nut Cookies

  1 cup chopped dates

  $^1/_2$ cup water

1 $^3/_4$ cups all-purpose flour

  $^1/_2$ teaspoon baking powder

  $^1/_8$ teaspoon salt

  $^1/_2$ cup butter, softened

  $^1/_2$ cup packed dark brown sugar

  1 egg

  2 teaspoons rum extract

  $^1/_2$ cup walnut pieces, chopped

Soak dates in water in small bowl at least 30 minutes or up to 2 hours.

Preheat oven to 350°F. Grease cookie sheets. Combine flour, baking powder and salt in medium bowl.

Beat butter in large bowl at medium speed until smooth. Gradually beat in brown sugar; increase speed to high and beat until light and fluffy. Beat in egg and rum extract until fluffy. Gradually stir in flour mixture alternately with date mixture, mixing just until combined after each addition. Stir in walnuts until blended.

Drop level tablespoonfuls of dough about 1$^1/_2$ inches apart onto prepared cookie sheets. Bake 14 minutes or until just set. Transfer to wire racks to cool completely. Store in airtight container.   *Makes 24 cookies*

Date-Nut Cookies

Fruitcake Cookies

$^1/_2$ cup butter, softened

$^3/_4$ cup sugar

$^1/_2$ cup milk

1 egg

2 tablespoons orange juice

1 tablespoon vinegar

2 cups all-purpose flour

1 teaspoon baking powder

$^1/_2$ teaspoon baking soda

$^1/_4$ teaspoon salt

$^1/_2$ cup chopped walnuts

$^1/_2$ cup chopped candied mixed fruit

$^1/_2$ cup raisins

$^1/_4$ cup chopped dried pineapple

Powdered sugar

Preheat oven to 350°F. Grease cookie sheets. Beat butter and sugar in large bowl until creamy. Beat in milk, egg, orange juice and vinegar until blended. Mix in flour, baking powder, baking soda and salt. Stir in walnuts, mixed fruit, raisins and pineapple. Drop rounded tablespoonfuls of dough 2 inches apart onto prepared cookie sheets.

Bake 12 to 14 minutes until lightly browned around edges. Cool 2 minutes on cookie sheets. Remove to wire racks; cool completely. Dust with powdered sugar. Store in airtight container.

Makes about 2$^1/_2$ dozen cookies

Golden Kolacky

   $^1/_2$ cup butter, softened

   4 ounces cream cheese, softened

   1 cup all-purpose flour

   Fruit preserves

Combine butter and cream cheese in large bowl; beat until smooth. Gradually add flour to butter mixture, blending until mixture forms soft dough. Divide dough in half; wrap each half in plastic wrap. Refrigerate until firm.

Preheat oven to 375°F. Roll out dough, half at a time, on floured surface to $^1/_8$-inch thickness. Cut into 3-inch squares. Spoon 1 teaspoon preserves in center of each square. Bring up two opposite corners to center; pinch together tightly to seal. Fold sealed tip to one side; pinch to seal. Place 1 inch apart on ungreased cookie sheets. Bake 10 to 15 minutes or until lightly browned. Remove to cooling racks; cool completely.

Makes about 2$^1/_2$ dozen cookies

Anna's Icing Oatmeal Sandwich Cookies

COOKIES

3/4 Butter Flavor* CRISCO® Stick or 3/4 cup Butter Flavor* CRISCO® all-vegetable shortening plus additional for greasing

1 1/4 cups firmly packed light brown sugar

1 egg

1/3 cup milk

1 1/2 teaspoons vanilla

3 cups quick oats, uncooked

1 cup all-purpose flour

1/2 teaspoon baking soda

1/2 teaspoon salt

FROSTING

2 cups confectioners' sugar

1/4 Butter Flavor* CRISCO® Stick or 1/4 cup Butter Flavor* CRISCO all-vegetable shortening

1/2 teaspoon vanilla

Milk

*Butter Flavor Crisco is artificially flavored.

1. Heat oven to 350°F. Grease baking sheets with shortening. Place sheets of foil on countertop for cooling cookies.

2. For cookies, combine 3/4 cup shortening, brown sugar, egg, milk and vanilla in large bowl. Beat at medium speed of electric mixer until well blended.

Anna's Icing Oatmeal Sandwich Cookies

3. Combine oats, flour, baking soda and salt. Mix into creamed mixture at low speed just until blended.

4. Drop rounded measuring tablespoonfuls of dough 2 inches apart onto prepared baking sheets.

5. Bake one sheet at a time at 375°F for 10 to 12 minutes, or until lightly browned. *Do not overbake.* Cool 2 minutes on baking sheet. Remove cookies to foil to cool completely.

6. For frosting, combine confectioners' sugar, shortening and vanilla in medium bowl. Beat at low speed, adding enough milk for good spreading consistency. Spread on bottoms of half the cookies. Top with remaining cookies.

Makes about 16 sandwich cookies

Checkerboard Bars

$^1/_2$ cup hazelnuts ($2^1/_2$ ounces)

4 ounces bittersweet or semisweet chocolate candy bar, broken into pieces

$2^1/_4$ cups all-purpose flour

$^1/_2$ teaspoon baking powder

$^1/_4$ teaspoon salt

$^3/_4$ cup butter, softened

$^3/_4$ cup sugar

2 eggs

1 teaspoon vanilla

Preheat oven to 350°F. To remove skins from hazelnuts, spread in single layer on baking sheet. Bake 10 to 12 minutes until toasted and skins begin to flake off; let cool slightly. Wrap hazelnuts in heavy kitchen towel; rub against towel to remove as much of skins as possible.

Place hazelnuts in food processor; process until finely chopped, but not pasty. Melt chocolate in small bowl over very hot water, stirring until smooth.

Combine flour, baking powder and salt in medium bowl. Beat butter and sugar in large bowl with electric mixer at medium speed until light and fluffy. Beat in 1 egg and vanilla. Gradually add flour mixture; beat well.

Reserve $1^1/_4$ cups dough. Stir chocolate and nuts into remaining dough. Wrap both doughs in plastic wrap and refrigerate 20 minutes.

Unwrap and roll out chocolate dough on lightly floured surface to $^1/_3$-inch thickness with floured rolling pin. Cut dough into twelve $4 \times ^3/_4$-inch strips. Reroll scraps as necessary, until all dough has been cut into strips. Repeat process with vanilla dough.

To assemble, beat remaining egg in small dish. Place one strip of chocolate dough on sheet of plastic wrap. Brush edge with egg. Place one strip of vanilla dough next to chocolate dough. Brush edge with egg. Repeat with one more chocolate strip and one more vanilla strip to make bottom layer. Brush top with egg.

Prepare second row by stacking strips on first row, alternating vanilla dough over chocolate and chocolate over vanilla dough. Brush edge of each strip and top layer with egg. Repeat with third row to complete 1 checkerboard bar. Repeat entire process with remaining dough strips to complete second checkerboard bar. Cover with plastic wrap; refrigerate 1 hour or until firm enough to slice.

Preheat oven to 350°F. Grease cookie sheets. Cut checkerboard bar crosswise with long, sharp knife into ¼-inch slices. Place 2 inches apart on prepared cookie sheets.

Bake 10 to 12 minutes or until set. Cool cookies on cookie sheets 2 minutes. Remove cookies with spatula to wire racks; cool completely. Store tightly covered at room temperature or freeze up to 3 months.

Makes 2 dozen bars

When a recipe calls for greased cookie sheets, use shortening or nonstick cooking spray for the best results. Butter or margarine may burn and cause the cookies to be too dark on the bottom.

Classic Refrigerator Sugar Cookies

1 cup butter, softened

1 cup sugar

1 egg

1 teaspoon vanilla

2 cups all-purpose flour

2 teaspoons baking powder

Dash nutmeg

$^1/_4$ cup milk

Colored sprinkles or melted semisweet chocolate* (optional)

*To dip 24 cookies, melt 1 cup chocolate chips in small saucepan over very low heat until smooth.

Beat butter in large bowl with electric mixer at medium speed until smooth. Add sugar; beat until well blended. Add egg and vanilla; beat until well blended.

Combine flour, baking powder and nutmeg in medium bowl. Add flour mixture and milk alternately to butter mixture, beating at low speed after each addition until well blended.

The five basic types of cookies include drop, bar, refrigerator (also called slice-and-bake), shaped and rolled (also called cutouts). These types are determined by the consistency of the dough and how it is formed into cookies.

Shape dough into 2 logs, each about 2 inches in diameter and 6 inches long. Roll logs in colored sprinkles, if desired, coating evenly (about ¼ cup sprinkles per roll). Or, leave rolls plain and decorate with melted chocolate after baking. Wrap each roll in plastic wrap. Refrigerate 2 to 3 hours or overnight.

Preheat oven to 350°F. Grease cookie sheets. Cut logs into ¼-inch-thick slices; place 1 inch apart on prepared cookie sheets. (Keep unbaked logs and sliced cookies chilled until ready to bake.)

Bake 8 to 10 minutes or until edges are golden brown. Transfer to wire racks to cool.

Dip plain cookies in melted chocolate or drizzle chocolate over cookies with fork or spoon, if desired. Set cookies on wire racks until chocolate is set. Store in airtight container.   *Makes about 48 cookies*

Classic Refrigerator Sugar Cookies

Golden Gingersnaps

1 package DUNCAN HINES® Golden Sugar Cookie Mix

1 egg

1 tablespoon water

1 tablespoon light molasses

1 1/2 teaspoons ground ginger

1 teaspoon ground cinnamon

1/2 teaspoon baking soda

1/4 cup granulated sugar

1 tablespoon milk

1/3 cup finely chopped pecans

Preheat oven to 375°F. Grease cookie sheets.

Combine cookie mix, egg, water, molasses, ginger, cinnamon and baking soda in large bowl. Stir until thoroughly blended. Drop by level tablespoonfuls into sugar. Roll to completely cover. Place 2 inches apart on prepared cookie sheets. Flatten slightly with bottom of drinking glass. Brush tops lightly with milk. Sprinkle with pecans. Bake 9 minutes for chewy cookies or 10 minutes for crisp cookies. Cool 2 minutes on cookie sheets. Remove to cooling racks. Cool completely. Store in airtight container. *Makes 3 dozen cookies*

Golden Gingersnaps

Banana Chocolate Chip Softies

1 $1/4$ cups all-purpose flour

1 teaspoon baking powder

$1/2$ teaspoon salt

$1/3$ cup butter, softened

$1/3$ cup granulated sugar

$1/3$ cup firmly packed light brown sugar

1 ripe, medium banana, mashed

1 large egg

1 teaspoon vanilla

1 cup milk chocolate chips

$1/2$ cup coarsely chopped walnuts (optional)

Preheat oven to 375°F. Lightly grease cookie sheets.

Place flour, baking powder and salt in small bowl; stir to combine.

Beat butter, granulated sugar and brown sugar in large bowl with electric mixer at medium speed until light and fluffy. Beat in banana, egg and vanilla. Add flour mixture. Beat at low speed until well blended. Stir in chips and walnuts with mixing spoon. (Dough will be soft.)

Drop rounded teaspoonfuls of dough 2 inches apart onto prepared cookie sheets.

Bake 9 to 11 minutes or until edges are golden brown. Let cookies stand on cookie sheets 2 minutes. Remove cookies with spatula to wire racks; cool completely. Store tightly covered at room temperature. These cookies do not freeze well.   *Makes about 3 dozen cookies*

Banana Chocolate Chip Softies

Old-Fashioned Desserts

Special occasions or any day, Grandma's desserts were not to be missed. Use Grandma's secret and keep the whole family at the table with your own irresistible homemade desserts.

Coconut Jam Cake

  1 package (2-layer size) yellow cake mix
  1 package (7 ounces) BAKER'S® ANGEL FLAKE Coconut,
    divided
  $^1/_2$ cup strawberry jam
  1 tub (8 ounces) COOL WHIP® Whipped Topping, thawed
  $^1/_2$ cup apricot jam
    Sliced fresh strawberries
    Canned apricot halves, drained
    Fresh mint leaves

HEAT oven to 350°F.

PREPARE and bake cake mix as directed on package for 2 (9-inch) round cake layers, gently stirring 1 cup of the coconut into batter just before pouring into pans. Cool 10 minutes; remove from pans. Cool completely on wire racks.

PLACE 1 cake layer on serving plate; spread top with strawberry jam. Spread $^3/_4$ cup of the whipped topping over jam; top with second cake layer. Spread top of cake with apricot jam. Frost top and sides of cake with remaining whipped topping. Pat remaining coconut onto sides of cake. Garnish with fruit and mint just before serving.

REFRIGERATE until ready to serve.   *Makes 12 servings*

Honey Pumpkin Pie

1 can (16 ounces) solid pack pumpkin

1 cup evaporated low-fat milk

³/₄ cup honey

3 eggs, slightly beaten

2 tablespoons all-purpose flour

1 teaspoon ground cinnamon

¹/₂ teaspoon ground ginger

¹/₂ teaspoon rum extract

Pastry for single 9-inch pie crust

Combine all ingredients except pastry in large bowl; beat until well blended. Pour into pastry-lined 9-inch pie plate. Bake at 400°F 45 minutes or until knife inserted near center comes out clean.

Makes 8 servings

Favorite recipe from **National Honey Board**

Related to the squash, the pumpkin is a member of the gourd family. The word is derived from the French word pompion *and the Greek word* pepon *meaning "cooked by the sun."*

Honey Pumpkin Pie

Blueberry Dream Fritters

Vegetable oil
$^1/_2$ cup whipping cream
1 egg
1 teaspoon vanilla
1 cup self-rising flour
$^1/_3$ cup self-rising cornmeal
$^1/_3$ cup granulated sugar
$1^1/_2$ cups fresh blueberries
Powdered sugar

1. Heat 2 inches oil in large heavy skillet to 375°F on deep-fat thermometer.

2. Meanwhile, combine cream, egg and vanilla in small bowl.

3. Combine flour, cornmeal and granulated sugar in large bowl. Stir in cream mixture just until moistened. Fold in blueberries.

4. Carefully drop batter by heaping tablespoonfuls into hot oil. Fry until golden brown, turning once. Drain well on paper towels. Sprinkle with powdered sugar; serve immediately. *Makes 12 fritters*

Prep and Cook Time: 20 minutes

Blueberry Dream Fritters

Orange Carrot Cake

1 cup margarine or butter, softened

1 cup GRANDMA'S® Molasses Unsulphured

4 eggs

1/2 cup orange juice

1 cup all-purpose flour

1 cup whole wheat flour

2 teaspoons baking soda

1 teaspoon ground cinnamon

1/2 teaspoon salt

2 cups shredded carrots

1/2 cup chopped walnuts

FROSTING

1 package (3 ounces) cream cheese, softened

2 tablespoons margarine or butter, softened

1 1/2 cups powdered sugar

1 teaspoon grated orange peel

Heat oven to 350°F. Grease two 8- or 9-inch round cake pans. In large bowl, combine margarine, molasses, eggs and orange juice; mix well. Stir in flours, baking soda, cinnamon and salt; mix well. Stir in carrots and walnuts. Pour into prepared pans. Bake at 350°F 30 to 35 minutes or until toothpick inserted in centers comes out clean. Cool 15 minutes; remove from pans. Cool completely.

In small bowl, combine all frosting ingredients; beat until smooth. Place one cake layer on serving plate; spread top with frosting. Top with second layer; spread top with frosting. If desired, garnish with additional orange peel and walnuts. *Makes 12 servings*

Baker's® Wellesley Fudge Cake

4 squares BAKER'S® Unsweetened Baking Chocolate

1³/₄ cups sugar, divided

¹/₂ cup water

1²/₃ cups flour

1 teaspoon baking soda

¹/₄ teaspoon salt

¹/₂ cup (1 stick) butter *or* margarine, softened

3 eggs

³/₄ cup milk

1 teaspoon vanilla

HEAT oven to 350°F. Grease and flour 2 (9-inch) round cake pans.

MICROWAVE chocolate, ¹/₂ cup sugar and water in large microwavable bowl on HIGH 1 to 2 minutes or until chocolate is almost melted, stirring halfway through heating time. Stir until chocolate is completely melted. Cool to lukewarm.

MIX flour, baking soda and salt; set aside. Beat butter and remaining 1¹/₄ cups sugar in large bowl with electric mixer on medium speed until light and fluffy. Add eggs, one at a time, beating well after each addition. Add flour mixture alternately with milk, beating after each addition until smooth. Stir in chocolate mixture and vanilla. Pour into prepared pans.

BAKE 30 to 35 minutes or until cake springs back when lightly touched. Cool 10 minutes; remove from pans. Cool completely on wire racks. Frost as desired.   *Makes 12 servings*

Prep Time: 30 minutes
Bake Time: 35 minutes

Cranberry Apple Crisp

$^1/_3$ to $^1/_2$ cup granulated sugar

3 tablespoons ARGO® or KINGSFORD'S® Corn Starch

1 teaspoon ground cinnamon

$^1/_2$ teaspoon ground nutmeg

5 to 6 cups cubed peeled tart apples

1 cup fresh or frozen cranberries

$^1/_2$ cup KARO® Light Corn Syrup

1 teaspoon grated orange peel

TOPPING

$^1/_2$ cup chopped walnuts or uncooked oats

$^1/_3$ cup packed brown sugar

$^1/_4$ cup all-purpose flour

$^1/_4$ cup ($^1/_2$ stick) MAZOLA® Margarine or butter

1. Preheat oven to 350°F.

2. In large bowl combine granulated sugar, corn starch, cinnamon and nutmeg. Add apples, cranberries, corn syrup and orange peel; toss to mix well. Spoon into shallow 2-quart baking dish.

3. For Topping, combine nuts, brown sugar and flour. With pastry blender or 2 knives, cut in margarine until mixture resembles very coarse crumbs. Sprinkle over cranberry mixture.

4. Bake 50 minutes or until apples are tender and juices that bubble up in center are shiny and clear. Cool slightly; serve warm.

Makes 6 to 8 servings

Cranberry Apple Crisp

Amaretto Coconut Cream Pie

¹/₄ cup flaked coconut

1 container (8 ounces) thawed nondairy whipped topping, divided

1 container (8 ounces) coconut cream-flavored or vanilla-flavored yogurt

¹/₄ cup amaretto liqueur

1 package (4-serving size) instant coconut pudding and pie filling mix

1 prepared (9-inch) graham cracker pie crust

Fresh strawberries and mint leaves (optional)

Preheat oven to 350°F. To toast coconut, place on baking sheet. Bake 4 to 5 minutes or until golden brown, stirring frequently. Cool completely.

Place 2 cups whipped topping, yogurt and amaretto in large bowl. Add pudding mix. Beat with wire whisk or electric mixer on low speed, 1 to 2 minutes or until thickened.

Pour pudding mixture into crust; spread remaining whipped topping over filling. Sprinkle with toasted coconut. Garnish with fresh strawberries and mint leaves, if desired. Refrigerate. *Makes 8 servings*

Amaretto Coconut Cream Pie

Sour Cream Pound Cake

1 orange

1 cup butter, softened

2³/₄ cups sugar

1 tablespoon vanilla

6 eggs

3 cups all-purpose flour

¹/₂ teaspoon salt

¹/₄ teaspoon baking soda

1 cup sour cream

Citrus Topping (recipe follows)

Preheat oven to 325°F. Grease 10-inch tube pan. Finely grate colored portion of orange peel. Measure 2 teaspoons orange peel; set aside. Beat butter in large bowl with electric mixer at medium speed until creamy, scraping down side of bowl once. Gradually add sugar, beating until light and fluffy. Beat in vanilla and orange peel. Add eggs, 1 at a time, beating 1 minute after each addition. Combine flour, salt and baking soda in small bowl. Add to butter mixture alternately with sour cream, beginning and ending with flour mixture. Beat well after each addition. Pour into prepared pan. Bake 1 hour 15 minutes or until wooden toothpick inserted in center comes out clean.

Meanwhile, prepare Citrus Topping. Spoon over hot cake; cool in pan 15 minutes. Remove from pan to wire rack; cool completely.

Makes 10 to 12 servings

Citrus Topping

2 oranges

2 teaspoons salt

Water

$^1/_2$ cup sugar, divided

$^1/_3$ cup lemon juice

1 teaspoon vanilla

With citrus zester or vegetable peeler, remove colored peel, not white pith, from oranges. Measure $^1/_3$ cup orange peel. Cut oranges in half. Squeeze juice from oranges into measuring cup or small bowl. Measure $^1/_3$ cup orange juice. Combine orange peel and salt in medium saucepan. Add enough water to cover. Bring to a boil over high heat. Boil 2 minutes. Drain in fine-meshed sieve. Return orange peel to saucepan. Add orange juice and $^1/_4$ cup sugar to saucepan. Bring to a boil over high heat. Reduce heat; simmer 10 minutes. Remove from heat. Add remaining $^1/_4$ cup sugar, lemon juice and vanilla; stir until smooth.

It used to be that a proper pound cake was made from a pound of butter, a pound of flour, a pound of eggs and a pound of sugar. Today, although the same ingredients are used, the proportions have changed considerably.

Raspberry Shortcakes

1 1/2 cups frozen whole raspberries, divided

  6 tablespoons sugar, divided

  1 cup all-purpose flour

  1 teaspoon baking powder

1/4 teaspoon baking soda

  1 tablespoon margarine

  1 egg white

1/3 cup evaporated skim milk

1/4 teaspoon almond extract

3/4 cup low fat cottage cheese

  1 teaspoon lemon juice

Preheat oven to 450°F. Spray baking sheet with nonstick cooking spray.

Toss 1 1/4 cups raspberries with 2 tablespoons plus 1 1/2 teaspoons sugar; set aside. Mix flour, 2 tablespoons sugar, baking powder and baking soda in medium bowl. Cut in margarine with pastry blender; set aside. Beat egg white, milk and almond extract in small bowl; add to flour mixture and mix lightly. Knead slightly on lightly floured board. Roll out to 1/2-inch thickness. Cut out 8 biscuits with 2 1/2-inch biscuit cutter. Place biscuits on prepared baking sheet. Bake 10 minutes or until lightly browned.

Meanwhile, place cottage cheese, remaining 1 1/2 teaspoons sugar and lemon juice in food processor; process until smooth. Fold in remaining 1/4 cup raspberries. To serve, split biscuits in half and place each bottom half on individual dish. Top each with 2 tablespoons reserved raspberries and 1 tablespoon cheese mixture. Cover with biscuit top. Spoon remaining reserved raspberries and cheese mixture over tops. *Makes 8 servings*

Favorite recipe from **The Sugar Association, Inc.**

Raspberry Shortcake

ACKNOWLEDGMENTS

The publisher would like to thank the companies and organizations listed below for the use of their recipes and photographs in this publication.

American Lamb Council

Bestfoods

Birds Eye®

Bob Evans®

Campbell Soup Company

ConAgra Grocery Products Company

Duncan Hines® and Moist Deluxe® are registered trademarks of Aurora Foods Inc.

Filippo Berio Olive Oil

Grandma's® is a registered trademark of Mott's, Inc.

Hebrew National®

Hillshire Farm®

Kraft Foods, Inc.

Lipton®

Michigan Apple Committee

National Fisheries Institute

National Honey Board

The Procter & Gamble Company

Reckitt & Colman Inc.

Riviana Foods Inc.

The Sugar Association, Inc.

VOLUME MEASUREMENTS (dry)

1/8 teaspoon = 0.5 mL
1/4 teaspoon = 1 mL
1/2 teaspoon = 2 mL
3/4 teaspoon = 4 mL
1 teaspoon = 5 mL
1 tablespoon = 15 mL
2 tablespoons = 30 mL
1/4 cup = 60 mL
1/3 cup = 75 mL
1/2 cup = 125 mL
2/3 cup = 150 mL
3/4 cup = 175 mL
1 cup = 250 mL
2 cups = 1 pint = 500 mL
3 cups = 750 mL
4 cups = 1 quart = 1 L

VOLUME MEASUREMENTS (fluid)

1 fluid ounce (2 tablespoons) = 30 mL
4 fluid ounces (1/2 cup) = 125 mL
8 fluid ounces (1 cup) = 250 mL
12 fluid ounces (1 1/2 cups) = 375 mL
16 fluid ounces (2 cups) = 500 mL

WEIGHTS (mass)

1/2 ounce = 15 g
1 ounce = 30 g
3 ounces = 90 g
4 ounces = 120 g
8 ounces = 225 g
10 ounces = 285 g
12 ounces = 360 g
16 ounces = 1 pound = 450 g

DIMENSIONS

1/16 inch = 2 mm
1/8 inch = 3 mm
1/4 inch = 6 mm
1/2 inch = 1.5 cm
3/4 inch = 2 cm
1 inch = 2.5 cm

OVEN TEMPERATURES

250°F = 120°C
275°F = 140°C
300°F = 150°C
325°F = 160°C
350°F = 180°C
375°F = 190°C
400°F = 200°C
425°F = 220°C
450°F = 230°C

BAKING PAN SIZES

Utensil	Size in Inches/Quarts	Metric Volume	Size in Centimeters
Baking or	8×8×2	2 L	20×20×5
Cake Pan	9×9×2	2.5 L	23×23×5
(square or	12×8×2	3 L	30×20×5
rectangular)	13×9×2	3.5 L	33×23×5
Loaf Pan	8×4×3	1.5 L	20×10×7
	9×5×3	2 L	23×13×7
Round Layer	8×1½	1.2 L	20×4
Cake Pan	9×1½	1.5 L	23×4
Pie Plate	8×1¼	750 mL	20×3
	9×1¼	1 L	23×3
Baking Dish	1 quart	1 L	—
or Casserole	1½ quart	1.5 L	—
	2 quart	2 L	—